P9-DTN-819

With special thanks

To Martin Kerr and Amy Schneider for beautiful book design.

To Helen Exley for believing in my work and your constant wise counsel throughout this project.

To my husband Jim, for everything.

Dedication: To Brent and Emily

Published in 2002 by Helen Exley Giftbooks in Great Britain.
16 Chalk Hill, Watford, Herts WD19 4BG, UK

Published in 2003 by Helen Exley Giftbooks LLC in the USA.
185 Main Street, Spencer, MA 01562, USA

www.helenexleygiftbooks.com

12 11 10 9 8 7 6 5 4

ISBN 978-1-86187-419-1

Edited by Helen Exley. Printed in China.

Written and illustrated by Susan Squellati Florence
www.susanflorence.com

Helen Exley Giftbooks cover the most powerful of all human relationships: love between couples, the bonds within families and between friends. No expense is spared in making sure that each book is as thoughtful and meaningful a gift as it is possible to create: good to give, good to receive. You have the result in your hands. If you have loved it — tell others! We'd rather put the money into more good books than spend it on advertising. There is no power on earth like the word-of-mouth recommendation of friends.

TAKE TIME ALONE
The gift of being with yourself

WRITTEN & ILLUSTRATED BY

Susan Squellati Florence

A HELEN EXLEY GIFTBOOK

*O*ur lives are so busy. Full of people and things to do. Our days are chaotic and confusing trying to get it all done. We know we need our own personal space. We ache to get away.

This book is about taking time to be with your self. It can be more important to be with your own self than to be with others. It is as important to be in "your world" as it is to be in "the world".

But it is hard to take time alone. We feel we are wasting time. There are parts of our lives we would rather not think about, so we keep busy. By taking time alone we can look at unresolved problems and be in touch with our sadness.

By being with all the different parts of ourselves,
we will grow and become more whole.

What we find within ourselves, when we take
time alone, is enormous. We can rediscover who
we really are. We look within and see the things
that are precious and meaningful to our lives.
We realize our hopes and dreams. We are
nourished by just "being". We find a sense of calm
that renews us.

I hope each day will bring you time alone with
someone wonderful... you!

When you take time alone
you discover the path
that goes deep
into yourself.

When you take time alone
you hear the voice
of your heart
speaking in silence.

When you take time alone
you leave the distractions
of the day...
and enter the secret garden
of your soul.

This is where
the deepest part of who you are
awaits you.

*This is where
all that you love is blooming.*

This, too, is where

your sorrow has been planted...

and unresolved problems

grow like tangled vines.

*Be brave enough
and willing to go alone
into the garden
of your self.*

You will see there

all the beautiful parts

of who you are.

Here in the garden

    you will have time to work

the sacred soil

      of your inner life.

You can clear the weeds
that have overgrown your dreams
and begin to nurture them again.

*You may uncover
and face the fears
buried long ago.*

You may be surprised to see

that what is important to you

has been neglected.

You will water the flowers
of your sadness
and become aware
of their gentle beauty.

You will begin to open up
the gnarled vines of problems
letting light shine through them.

Here in the quiet
you will be able to sit
and do nothing.

Just breathe.

You may sense you are with
a part of yourself
that you have forgotten.
The one who knows
what you want...
not what others want of you.
The one who can listen
to the voice within you.

You will be one
with all that you are.

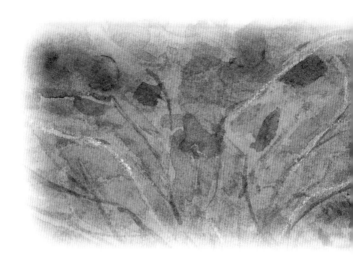

This garden is awaiting you.
Even if it has been untended,
even if you've left it far behind.

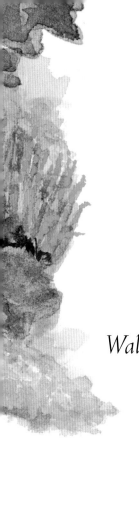

*Walk into the garden
of your self.*

Tend the beautiful parts
of yourself growing there.

Cherish the life
you have been entrusted with.

*Plant the seeds
of new hopes and dreams.*

*Rest and listen
to the deep and joyful song
of your soul.*

Take time alone.
Solitude will nourish you.

You will be filled...

not with what you have longed for

but with the absence

of longing itself.

Solitude
will renew you
and like morning sunlight
on flowers,
touch you with peace.

ABOUT THE AUTHOR

Susan Squellati Florence

The well loved and collected greeting cards of Susan Florence
have sold hundreds of millions of copies in the last
three decades. Her giftbooks have sold over one and a half
million copies.

  With words of gentle wisdom and original paintings, Susan
Florence brings her unique style to all her gift products and
her readers have written time and again to thank her and tell
her how the books were a profound help to them. People have
told Susan that her words speak to them of what they cannot
say... but what they feel.

  Susan Florence's completely new collection of giftbooks in
The Journeys Series invites the readers to pause and look
deeply into their lives. "We all need more time to rediscover
and reflect on what is meaningful and important in our own

lives... and what brings us joy and beauty. Writing these books in The Journeys Series *has helped me understand more fully the value of love and acceptance in helping us through the difficult times as we journey through life."*

Susan lives with her husband, Jim, in Ojai, California. They have two grown children, Brent and Emily.

THE JOURNEYS SERIES